When to Get My Kid a Phone

Navigating the Tensions

Drew Hill

New Growth Press

newgrowthpress.com

New Growth Press, Greensboro, NC 27404
newgrowthpress.com
Copyright © 2020 by Drew Hill

Cover Design: Tom Temple
Interior Design and Typesetting: Gretchen Logterman

ISBN: 978-1-64507-096-2 (Print)
ISBN: 978-1-64507-097-9 (eBook)

Library of Congress Cataloging-in-Publication Data

Names: Hill, Drew, author.
Title: When to get my kid a phone : navigating the tensions / Drew Hill.
Description: Greensboro, NC : New Growth Press, 2020. | Summary: "Thoughtful parents wonder how to steward technology well and protect their children from potential pitfalls. When is the right time to give your child access to such powerful tools?"-- Provided by publisher.
Identifiers: LCCN 2020015018 (print) | LCCN 2020015019 (ebook) | ISBN 9781645070962 (print) | ISBN 9781645070979 (ebook)
Subjects: LCSH: Parenting--Religious aspects--Christianity. | Child rearing--Religious aspects--Christianity. | Technology--Religious aspects--Christianity. | Smartphones.
Classification: LCC BV4529 .H555 2020 (print) | LCC BV4529 (ebook) | DDC 248.8/45--dc23
LC record available at https://lccn.loc.gov/2020015018
LC ebook record available at https://lccn.loc.gov/2020015019

Printed in South Korea

27 26 25 24 23 22 21 20   1 2 3 4 5

Determining when your child gets a smartphone will be one of the most complicated yet critical decisions you'll ever make. While this minibook will *not* give you an exact number for that "magical appropriate age," it will give you a *one-word answer* for how to wisely navigate the tensions of this touchy topic.

Over the past decade, I've counseled countless parents who have navigated this road and who, like you, desire to steward technology well and to protect their kids from potential pitfalls. I've learned much from watching a couple of our best friends walk through this "phone decision" with their middle schooler Ty[1]. Instead of being controlled by fear and simply forbidding access to all electronic devices, they've become some of the most intentional parents I've ever seen in regard to handling technology. Even still, they wrestle with worrying about not doing enough or doing it wrong.

When Ty was in fourth grade, his parents began an open and continuing conversation around the topic. By sixth grade, he was one of the only kids among his friends without a phone. On his twelfth birthday, his parents gave Ty a used, older model of an iPhone. They made clear that this phone was not just a gift but also a responsibility; they were going to entrust him with this phone, but also monitor closely.

The phone was accompanied by a document they'd carefully thought through. It's shared here, with their permission.

We are excited to give you a phone,
because you have earned our trust!

We don't want you to:
- Miss out on the joy of worship
- Get stuck in a "Christian bubble"
- Be pushed outside of social circles
- Fear the world because it is broken

Instead, we want you to:
- Hear and speak truth
- Be in the world, but not of the world
- Connect with a group of friends
- Enter brokenness with wisdom

But we want to give it to you slowly,
walking alongside you, one step at a time.

Because misuse of phones can cause you to:
- Miss out on the joy of nature
- Miss out on the opportunity to create
- Avoid being alone, still, or quiet
- Become dependent on affirmation of others
- Only have shallow friendships
- Never learn to say uncomfortable things in person
- Become bound and burdened by shame
- Lack trust in your marriage
- View people as objects

And we want to help you:
- Enjoy God's creation (Psalm 19:1)
- Have fun being creative (Genesis 1)
- Find time to be alone, still, and quiet (Isaiah 30:15)
- Be rooted in your identity in Christ
  (Deuteronomy 33:12; 1 Peter 2:9)

- Find friends you can trust in hard times (Ecclesiastes 4:9–12)
- Speak with courage and vulnerability (Acts 4:13)
- Live freely and lightly (Matthew 11:28–30)
- Build trust (Malachi 2:16; 1 Corinthians 13:4–8)
- Maximize enjoyment of sex in marriage (Song of Solomon 4:10)

Your phone use will be gradual.

Here are the steps we will take together over a period of time.
- Begin with music and audio books
- Later, add calling and texting, initially just using Wi-Fi
- Eventually, add other apps and games
- Later, add internet and Siri
- Finally, allow social media use

Here is our family "phone protection plan."
- Kid phones will be shut down from 8 p.m. to 8 a.m.
- All phones stay in the charging station at night.
- Parents have full access to kid phones at all times.
- Lying or misuse of phone will result in immediate loss of phone.
- Parents make the rules, but kids have real input.

Notice how Ty's parents introduced initial privileges, then added more privileges over time. The short answer to the question of "When should I get my kid a phone?" is simply one word:

GRADUALLY!

Like Learning to Drive

When I was in middle school, I did something illegal.

Some Wednesday nights, after the church parking lot had cleared out, my dad let me get behind the wheel of our '88 Ford Taurus and practice driving before we headed home. I was only thirteen. A few years before that, he'd let me start cutting the grass with the riding mower. Almost every summer of my childhood we'd race go-karts at the Myrtle Beach Grand Prix. Due to all the practice, when I finally took "in-car" testing with my driving school instructor, I was a confident fifteen-year-old who easily passed and got my driver's permit.

After a year of navigating the main roads with my folks riding shotgun, April 18 finally arrived—my sixteenth birthday. It's a day I'll never forget, because it was the day I nervously rolled past a stop sign and failed my driving test. Is there anything more humiliating than going to school the day after your "sweet sixteen" and having everyone ask to see your new driver's license—the one that didn't exist?

I was able to take the driving test again the following day. I passed, but for the next four years my license had April 19 as the issue date, printed right beside my April 18 birthday—a constant reminder of my "sour sixteen."

Six months later, on October 30, I made another error in judgment and totaled my '84 Accord. After racing almost 100 mph down Interstate 40 and abruptly turning the wheel to get off an exit I'd missed, the car flipped three times and I ended up on a stretcher in an ambulance speeding to the ER. I spent that Halloween at home, in bed, with a shaved head full of staples from where the windshield glass had slashed my skull. It could've been a great costume if I'd been up for trick-or-treating.

It took me a month or so to get up the confidence to get back behind the wheel. It was another four months before my parents bought me another car.

I was eighteen when I got my first speeding ticket. When I was twenty-one, I got my second. But knock on wood, it's now been more than two decades since I've wrecked a car or gotten a ticket.

So, what does all this talk about driving have to do with phones? Think about it this way: *Could the journey behind the wheel be a map for you as you consider teaching your child how to maneuver a phone?*

Our culture understands that driving is a huge responsibility. As a result, there's a process in place that allows kids to gradually learn how to drive. Kids first get to ride with their parents and learn by watching. Then they get a taste of being behind a wheel, on mechanisms like go-karts and riding lawnmowers. Around the early teenage years, they take a class on the dangers of driving and have to pass a test. After that they get a year of required practice, driving with an adult riding in the passenger seat. Then (in some states) there's a provisional license that comes with restrictions such as curfew times and limitations on underage passengers in the vehicle. Finally, even after the full driving license has been granted, law enforcement still hands out costly consequences when infractions occur.

"Driver's Ed" for Phone Use

Much like driving, learning to use a phone is a weighty responsibility that also needs to be implemented by an intentional and gradual training process. For the remainder of this minibook, we'll lay out a *gradual* phone training process using this formula.

> Phase 1: You watch me do it.
> Phase 2: You do it with me.
> Phase 3: I watch you do it.
> Phase 4: You do it.

Phase 1: You watch me do it.

I recently visited a forty-year-old friend who is married with kids. Her father, Chuck, is battling dementia and now lives with her family. During that afternoon, I noticed that Chuck spent a majority of the time in his recliner reading the Bible. I asked his daughter if that was normal.

Her response is one I won't soon forget: "Yes. He does it daily. And he always has. When I remember my childhood, that right there is exactly how I remember my daddy. Every morning when I walked down the steps, he was always either reading God's Word or on his knees in prayer."

The most important way to help your child learn to use a phone is through modeling. Your kids are watching you and will imitate you, and that's a lot of pressure. They are paying attention to how you use your phone when driving, before bed, and at the dinner table. They are more aware than you realize. The best way to teach them healthy phone habits is for you to practice them yourself.

So, do you feel like you've already failed? Me too.

Navigating our phone usage is a constant and hard-fought battle. It's a struggle for adults and children alike to not become obsessed with scrolling through endless apps and wasting countless hours. One of the best ways we can instruct our kids in this realm is by inviting them into the war with us.

What if you asked your nine-year-old to sit beside you on the couch and talk about phones? What if you started with an apology and a confession? Think about how powerful it could be for your child to hear you say, "I'm sorry for the way I've allowed my phone to distract me from you, our family, and the Lord. Will you forgive me?"

What if you didn't stop there, but also asked them to help remind you the next time you ignore them by spending an hour playing Candy Crush? As they see you lead yourself through repentance, it opens the door for them to do the same.

To read more about healthy screen habits, I recommend some helpful resources. The first is *The Tech-Wise Family* by Andy Crouch. One of Andy's most helpful suggestions is to take a "screen sabbath" for one hour per day, one day per week, and one week per year. That simple practice alone will be a game-changer for your family, as you consider the role of technology in your life.

I also encourage you to read *The Common Rule: Habits of Purpose for an Age of Distraction* by Justin Earley. It's a great book to discuss as a family and offers eight practical habits you could immediately start implementing, such as "Scripture before screens" and limiting media to four hours per week. *Living into Focus* by Arthur Boers is another book packed with relatable stories and eye-opening wisdom. I personally underlined more than half the book.

The earlier you start having these conversations with your kids, the better. But if you feel like it's too late, know that it's not. While habits certainly become more difficult to change the older our children (or we) become, we have a God who loves transformation and who specializes in making broken things beautiful. Give the Lord a chance to show off!

Here's another idea: discuss Romans 12:1–2 as a family. How do we place our everyday habits, such as how we use our phones, before the Lord as an offering?

> Therefore, I urge you, brothers and sisters, in view of God's mercy, to offer your bodies as a living sacrifice, holy and pleasing to God—this is your true and proper worship. Do not conform to the pattern of this world, but be transformed by the renewing of your mind. Then you will be able to test and approve what God's will is—his good, pleasing and perfect will.

> So here's what I want you to do, God helping you: Take your everyday, ordinary life—your sleeping, eating, going-to-work, and walking-around life—and place it before God as an offering. Embracing what God does for you is the best thing you can do for him. Don't become so well-adjusted to your culture that you fit into it without even thinking. Instead, fix your attention on God. You'll be changed from the inside out. Readily recognize what he wants from you, and quickly respond to it. Unlike the

culture around you, always dragging you down to its level of immaturity, God brings the best out of you, develops well-formed maturity in you. (MSG)

In every "phone talk" you have with your kids, help them understand that the guardrails you've set up aren't ultimately about behavioral modification and just spending less time on a device. This isn't a simple scuffle over the merits and pitfalls of screen time. This is about a full-out war for our hearts. Our affections are formed by the things we give our attention to. What we look at shapes what we love. Invite your kids to join you in fixing your attention on God.

Phase 2: You do it with me.

Predictably, there will come a time when your child asks for a phone—but oddly enough, the "phone" part of the device is likely to be one of the least used features. They'll want to use it for playing games, taking pictures, listening to music, watching shows, shopping on Amazon, texting with friends, or using any of the more than two million apps on the App Store. Odds are that even if your child doesn't already have a phone, they've already experimented with using a device with similar features, such as a laptop, iPad, Kindle, Xbox, or AppleTV.

Your kids are using technology in some form already, and will continue to do so for the rest of their lives. If you're not helping them learn how to navigate these roads, who will? It seems like Siri, Google, Alexa, not to mention your child's peers, are happily up for the challenge, but is that who you want teaching your kids "driving lessons?"

What keeps us from engaging our kids in these discussions? Maybe our hesitancy stems from shame and guilt about how we've been manipulated by our own devices. Possibly it's fear of what opening this Pandora's box will do to our babies. Or could it just be that we are unaware of the pressing need to address these topics head-on and don't know how to guide our children through these complicated technological waters?

It's important to process your thoughts and feelings with your kids. Allow them to see you wrestling with weighty decisions and invite them into it with you. Ask them to pray for wisdom for you in this area, and spend time praying over your technological decisions together. Let them know that you are in this *with* them and that you are *for* them.

As you invite your kids into conversations about when and how to use technology, go over some "house rules" similar to what Ty's parents drafted. Let's look back over part of the document they gave Ty when they decided to first give him a phone:

- Begin with music and audio books
- Later, add calling and texting, initially just using Wi-Fi
- Eventually, add other apps and games
- Later, add internet and Siri
- Finally, allow social media use

Be clear with your kids that "over a period of time" could mean several years, but that you want to navigate that timeline together. The "music and audio books" privilege could be made available in sixth grade—but social media, maybe not until high school. Each child's maturity level is different, and the appropriate ages will be different for each step in the process. The reality is most of these privileges should likely be granted earlier than you are comfortable with, but later than your child desires.

Before presenting a document like this to your child, I'd recommend pulling together some wise friends and asking their input. Ask your youth pastor or parents who are in a stage of life ahead of you. Most of my friends who now have kids in college would tell you that they wish they had waited longer before giving their kids a phone. It's important to hear and to learn from their experiences.

Once you've prayed, read, had helpful conversations, and taken a lot of notes, then make sure to get on the same page with your spouse before talking to your child. (For those of you who are single parents, it's helpful to bring another adult into this conversation with you for backup and validation—a pastor, aunt, babysitter, grand-parent, coach, etc.)

Think of a fun way to present the phone and the plan to your child. Ty's parents took him to his favorite restaurant to mark the occasion, hoping it would under-score the significance of the moment. A kid's first phone is nothing to be taken lightly and it is a prime opportu-nity to speak truth to open ears. Ty's parents' actions and words indicated the coming season would be for shared phone usage and not for Ty to *own* the phone.

Since many peers don't have to share a phone with their parents, this might be a hard distinction for them to understand. Keep reminding them of the "whys." When you take driver's ed, you watch videos of people who have killed others by careless driving, drunk driving, and texting while driving. These stories are sobering reminders of the huge responsibility we have when sitting behind the wheel. Similarly, it would be helpful for your children to understand more of the responsibilities and dangers of having a phone.

There are plenty of online articles and videos about the consequences of unwise phone usage, but face-to-face testimonies will be the most powerful. Consider inviting some older teenagers, college students, or young adults to come over and share their stories with your kids. Many of my teenage friends could tell you stories about how they formed destructive habits from poor choices related to phones—about how they used to live freely and lightly but poor phone usage made them grow up too fast and filled their nights with sleepless anxiety. Much like with sex before marriage, I have lots of friends who say about getting a phone, "Oh, how I wish I would have waited." When your kids hear true stories from people they respect, it makes a difference in how carefully they approach this new responsibility.

Nonetheless, don't leave them with a sense of fear. Make sure the stories they hear also tell the truth of God's redemption and how he has worked through these trials. And just as God doesn't abandon us and leave us to drown in our despair, remind your kids that you are in this journey *with* them—and that's why this is a season of you learning to use a phone *together*!

Give your kids some practical examples of how this could play out. Maybe they are begging to join their friends on Instagram. Consider allowing them to create an account, but only you (the parent) know the password, and the app is only installed on your phone. They can only use it under your supervision. It's much like riding shotgun in a go-kart, where the parent drives until the child is forty-eight inches tall. This is a season for children to experience the thrill of the ride, but it is not yet the season for them to drive.

One of the main reasons your child will initially desire a phone is so they won't feel left out. It's hard when their friends are all texting and they feel like the oddball. One practical solution in the beginning is to get your child a Google Voice number. They can text and call through Google Voice on different devices, but you can log in to their account and be aware of all their activity, including the ability to read through their text threads.

One way you could communicate to your child that you're in it together is by submitting yourselves to some of the same guidelines you've given them. If a phone is "never to be used behind closed doors," tell them that you want to abide by that policy as well. Ask them to hold you accountable to plugging your phone in the kitchen at night, instead of taking it in your bedroom or bathroom. It changes the way your children view the battle when they know that you're both fighting on the same side.

Phase 3: I watch you do it.

There will eventually come a time when you'll give your child a device, and say something that may seem scary but is actually quite freeing:

"Courtney, we've been doing this phone thing together for a while now, and I'm so proud of how you've handled this responsibility. My job as your parent is to train you to become an adult and to live independently of me, so we've come to the next training phase in our phone journey. We're moving from the 'You do it with me' stage into 'I watch you do it.' And I have great confidence in you!"

Be careful not to quickly move into this stage if you can't say that last line: "and I have great confidence in you!" Would you let your child drive a car if you didn't think they had enough training and practice to do it? That's not saying you won't still be nervous, but it carries great weight when your kids are convinced you believe in them. Some parents will be hesitant to trust their kids but still need to proceed with entering this phase. Being as honest as you can, point out ways that your child has built trust and communicate confidence in them. When we do that, we cast vision over their future.

When I was in high school, I wrote an article for our local community newspaper. My grandmother drove all around town collecting copies of the paper and passing them out to her friends. My mom cut out the article and put it on our fridge. My dad put it on his office door at work. They made me believe I was a good writer. So, I wrote another newspaper article with even more confidence.

Likewise, in every interaction you have about the phone, keep communicating confidence and vision.

When they're wearing headphones and listening to music on the van ride to Christmas at Grandma's, don't just yell at them to "take off their headphones and be part of the family!" Instead, before the trip, pull them aside and come up with an agreed-upon screen usage plan for the drive:

> I know we're going to be in the van for a few hours and that you don't want to watch *Frozen* yet again with your younger siblings and would rather listen to music, but I also really value this family time and would love for us to spend more of the ride in conversation than staring at screens. I know it's easier to tune out and that talking to each other takes more effort, but I just want to know you more, because I think you're incredible, and I want us to fight for our relationships with each other. I want us to be a family that is close, that knows one another deeply, and that listens to each other well. And I know that deep down, you want that too.
>
> Your brother and sister look up to you so much and they would love if you would play "I Spy" with them for just ten minutes. Would you be willing to spend the first hour of the ride playing games and in conversation with us and to even put your phone in the glove compartment for that part of the trip? What if I gave you $10 that you could give as "prize money" for the games and we'll stop at a gas station in an hour and you buy your siblings some slushies? Then, after that, we can put on a DVD for your

siblings, and you can listen to music. How does that sound?

Communicating ahead of time is often way more effective than shameful correction in the heat of the moment. If you forget, maybe it's best to not fight that battle in the van but to wait a day or so and talk about it when things have calmed down.

This phase of you "watching them do it" is tricky unless you have set clear expectations upfront. Let's revisit the Instagram example from the previous section. During the "together phase," the social media apps were only on your phone. During this phase, you now give your child the freedom of having these apps on her own device. Note that this doesn't mean you are granting unsupervised free rein with social media use. At this stage you should still have the account passwords and still be able to log in and see activity. The parent still has the right to look at the child's phone at any time, and if inappropriate use is happening, you can delete the app.

Enforcement of these guidelines is going to feel painful to your teenager, but if you make rules that aren't carried out you're only hurting them more. Would you drive faster than the speed limit if there were no police officers who would give you a ticket and raise your insurance rates? Accountability offers us all the gift of safety. Communicate this idea ahead of time to your teenager; it will help him understand that you're not finding delight in being a detective, but that you're simply helping him learn to "drive safely." A speeding ticket is way better than a head-on collision.

Here again is an opportunity to invite someone you know to tell her story. Few things are more powerful than a personal testimony! Maybe you know someone who struggled with being bullied online or a business owner who didn't hire someone because of what he saw on a social media page. When we allow our kids to hear those stories, we help them connect the dots and see that their online behavior and social media interactions will have a significant influence on their future.

Again, please don't leave the conversation stuck in the fear of failure. Cast hopeful vision over their lives. Consider saying something like, "I have great confidence in you and because of Christ in you, you already have everything you need to face the curves in the road ahead. He won't leave you alone." But also acknowledge that they will fail, and that like you and me they'll probably get some speeding tickets and fender benders along the way. But when they do, respond with grace and remind them of the redemption of the cross and how the mercies of the Lord are new every day. This is a great opportunity to share the gospel with your children.

Phase 4: You do it.

This is the scariest phase for a parent. It's when you stare into the future and reckon with the inevitability of your children's independence from you. But this phase also has some perks. It's when your kids start paying their own phone bills and repairing their own cracked screens. But this is also when they have their own passwords. This is when you have to let go and trust the Lord. I recommend that this stage occurs within the final year or two of a teenager living at home. You want them making their first big phone mistakes while they're still living under your roof.

We've talked a lot about how important it is to hear other people's stories of failure and redemption around their relationships with phones. But in this stage, when maybe you have even more fear than with the other phases, take some time to remember your own story. What has God done in your own life? How has he brought dead things to life?

As you move into this stage, consider writing out some of your own story as a gift to your child. Maybe it involves your own failure with the phone, or maybe it's even more than that. Imagine how it might have been for you if your parents would have given you that gift of transparency? The reality is that no matter what you do, you can't prevent your kids from making bad decisions. You can guide them wisely, but your kids are sinners and they will sin. Their sin is not your weight to bear. Jesus already bore it for them on the cross. When they fail, you get to remind them of the power of Christ's blood shed on their behalf.

Teaching our kids about a godly use of technology is a microcosm of the overall trajectory of parenting. It's one of the many ways we surrender our hands-on oversight and bring our kids to the point where we release them to live as responsible adults before God. Ultimately, it's a chance for us to model a life of faith for our children. Through this process, we get to show them how to take our hands off the steering wheel and live with the confidence that God is our good forever Father.

Suggested Reading and Resources

- *Alongside: Loving Teenagers with the Gospel* by Drew Hill (see also AlongsideTeenagers.com)
- *The Tech-Wise Family* by Andy Crouch
- *12 Ways Your Phone Is Changing You* by Tony Reinke
- *Good Pictures, Bad Pictures* by Kristen A. Jenson and Debbie Fox
- Axis.org (sign up for "The Culture Translator," a free, weekly email that helps you stay in the know about relevant teenage culture)
- CovenantEyes.com
- Disney Circle (home Wi-Fi router with safety features)
- iPhone's "ScreenTime" settings make it easy for parents to remove the App Store and control what apps are allowed on the phone. It also allows you to schedule shut-down time for specific apps, as well as general phone use.
- For moms and dads seeking guidance about parental controls and filters on smartphones, the following websites offer helpful resources and tips:
  » Protectyoungminds.org
  » Protectyoungeyes.com
  » Axis.org (look for downloadable PDFs titled "A Parent's Guide to iOS" and "A Parent's Guide to Android")

A Sample Phone Agreement[2]

An agreement like this can be used at every stage in the process of giving your child a phone and is most effectively used when revisited often, especially at transitions between stages.

As I know that phones can be good things that are often misused—tempting us to act, talk, or think in ways that are not God-honoring—I agree to commit to the following:

1. I will strive to avoid gossip, bad-mouthing, and discouraging or unwholesome talk. (Ephesians 4:29)
2. I will guard my eyes and heart against images that dishonor God, knowing that pornography is real, readily available, and that I will be targeted by that industry in the hopes that I will become a regular customer. I am fully aware that nothing on the internet is truly private. I will not look at things that I wouldn't want my mother, father, or Sunday school teacher seeing. (Philippians 4:8)
3. I will never send or post a photo or video of someone without their permission. This includes siblings. (Luke 6:31)
4. I will not be so preoccupied with my phone that I ignore situations or people around me. I will remember that God has called me to love those around me, and that this is hard to do when I'm staring at a screen. (Ephesians 5:1–2)
5. Whenever possible, I will put my phone to good use as a tool of gospel outreach, encouragement, and care for others. (Matthew 5:16)
6. I will not send compromising photos of myself to anyone. If someone sends compromising photos to me,

I will take my phone directly to my parents without reply. (1 Corinthians 6:19–20)

7. I will continue to study and learn God's Word so that I have discernment on the internet, recognizing which ideas are biblical and which aren't. I acknowledge that most of the world's advice is directly opposed to what the Bible teaches, and I will be vigilant in clinging to the truth of the Bible above all else. (2 Timothy 3:16–17)

8. I understand that nothing on my phone is secret or private. My parents have apps that report my activity, and they will also regularly look through all of my content. This is one way that my parents help keep me safe and hold me accountable as a fellow Christian and beloved child. (Hebrews 10:23–24; 13:17)

I understand that this agreement before the Lord is between my parents and me. I know that in any area of life, temptation can only be overcome with the help of the Holy Spirit. So, I will rely on Christ, and I will remember that with the Holy Spirit's help, *no* temptation is too strong to resist (1 Corinthians 10:13; 2 Timothy 1:7). And when I do sin, I will remember that my sin is no match for the wonderful grace of my loving, compassionate God (Hebrews 4:15–16).

I know that my parents are a safe haven for me and that they understand the temptations that come with cell phones. I will not be afraid to talk with them about anything, and especially not something that is worrying me, upsetting me, convicting me, or scaring me.

Signed: _____

Date:_____

Endnotes

1. Names have been changed to respect privacy.
2. Used with permission from by Melissa Edgington, author of YourMomHasABlog.com.